I0458087

LESSONS FROM MY FATHER

LESSONS FROM MY FATHER

BRENDA ANDERSON

Copyright © 2025 by Brenda Anderson

All rights reserved. No part of this publication may be reproduced,
distributed, or transmitted in any form or by any means, including
photocopying, recording, or other electronic or mechanical meth-
ods, without the prior written permission of the publisher, except
in the case of brief quotations embodied in critical reviews and
certain other noncommercial uses permitted by copyright law.

Onion River Press
89 Church Street
Burlington, VT 05401
info@onionriverpress.com
www.onionriverpress.com

ISBN: 978-1-966607-19-9

Library of Congress Control Number: 2025920074

This book is dedicated to all the dads who thought their life lessons went unnoticed.

Contents

Introduction

I n today's world, where everything moves so quickly, there are days we forget to even breathe. Thank you for slowing down and sharing your time with me and my story. Sometimes it feels like life is spinning so fast that society has lost some of its values in the vortex. *Lessons from My Father* is a tribute to my dad and his old-fashioned Yankee way of thinking. The intent of this book is not to imply that my dad was better than yours or that he had all the answers. Growing up, I wished my father were different. I wanted him to be like everyone else's dad. I wanted him to dress nicer, talk more, and be more affluent. I wanted him to spend more time at home, to solve problems, and to be perfect. I wanted him to be just like Mike Brady from *The Brady Bunch* or Steven Douglas from *My Three Sons*. It took time and observation to realize no one has a TV dad.

As I spent more time in the adult world, I realized how lucky I was to have had a father like mine. I also learned that many people did not have a dad at all or chose not to cultivate a relationship with them. It would have been extremely helpful if my father had taught me how to change the oil in my car or explained why mice prefer my basement to the neighbors or showed me what poison ivy looks like in winter. Instead, he taught me much bigger things about the world, like respect, responsibility, and how to navigate this rocky road called life. Not all lessons came verbally. Many of his teachings came just from being around him. Let's call it "dad osmosis."

As you read this book, I hope you can absorb his words as I did. Read a bit, think a bit, do some journaling, think some more, and run it by your dog as you try to figure out how his tidbits of wisdom can work their way into your life. After each chapter, there are sections titled "Thoughts" with prompts where you can contemplate the topic more and write or journal if you chose to. There is even enough space to write down your own memories. The "Diary" pages are actual excerpts from my dad's diaries. The pages titled "Remembering Gus" are notes on sympathy cards that people shared with my mom, Kathryn, upon his passing. I invite you to take a deep breath, slow down, and retreat to a simpler time. Our world can always use a new perspective, and I believe the way in which my father viewed life is a worthy blueprint. I humbly share with you *Lessons from My Father*.

Meet Gus...

I had an amazing father named Gus. He was a strong man who stood about 6'2" and weighed around 230 pounds—though his weight fluctuated, depending on how much ice cream he had eaten that week. Except for weddings and funerals, you would find him in a plaid flannel shirt, denim overalls, work boots, and a cap. His huge hands bore scars and calluses from years of demanding work. He grew up on the family farm in North Central Massachusetts, not far from the borders of Vermont and New Hampshire, and, although fascinated by the world around him, he chose to stay at the homestead and continue working the land.

My dad's paternal family arrived on Ellis Island from Sweden. In Sweden, it was common to name your son after the king, so my grandfather became Philip Gustaf Adolph Johnson. My grandparents gave my dad the same name. Over time, everyone simply called him Gus.

A quiet man, Dad earned a living by following the seasons. In spring, there were sugar maples to tap. Even though you might find syrup on your pancakes simply delicious, the process of creating that syrup is anything but simple. It involves hours of hammering taps into the right place on the maple tree, hanging buckets with covers, gathering the sap that spills forth from the tree, and boiling it to the perfect consistency. Depending on the weather, the process of gathering sap may even need to be done on snowshoes! Only then is the sugary tree sap finally turned into liquid gold. The hot New England summers found him in the fields cutting and baling the tall grass into hay. He used it for his own dairy cows and sold some. In autumn, there was firewood to split and sell to help people prepare for the chilly winter ahead. When snow covered the ground, Dad would climb on his tractor and plow driveways. Year round, there were always dairy cows to milk, calves to feed, and equipment to repair.

Daily work continued from sunup to sundown with only an occasional break for "Fika," a traditional Swedish afternoon coffee time. It consists of strong coffee, a sweet snack, and an opportunity to socialize. My dad spoke softly but listened hard. Growing up, I remember young men staying with us for short periods. They were usually having issues at home with their families and needed a new environment where they could ponder life. My dad needed help on the farm, and he was a good listener, so it was a perfect match. I think the conversations they shared, and the lessons he relayed, were probably more valuable than any paycheck.

My dad did not communicate his thoughts much, but he was always interested in what other people thought. It was not unusual for him to read something in the newspaper or hear something on the radio and then call me or one of my siblings to ask for our opinion. Sometimes, like when the Red Sox made a trade, he wanted everyone's input!

He never held political office, never met the world's definition of "important," and never had a lot of money. My father was rich, however, in ways that really mattered. He knew everyone in town and their families. Our town had around six thousand people, so it was medium-sized by New England standards. The businesses were all small and locally owned, including the bank. There were no chain restaurants and no big box stores. A simple trip to town took hours as people stopped to chat with my dad. He greeted everyone with a firm handshake and a "how are your folks?" He treated everyone the same, whether they drove a Cadillac or rode a bicycle. He was a simple man who lived a simple life. The lessons he shared were honest and often life changing.

Though he was a man who lived simply, he kept a handwritten diary that he wrote in daily. He wrote about the work he performed on the farm each day, when and where he and my mom went out to lunch, the people he talked to, and the animals he encountered. These facts might not be important to anyone else, but on that day, they were important to him. The one constant in his diary was the weather. Even if there were no other notations for the day, he always posted the temperature. I can tell you with confidence that it was 28 degrees on the day he died. His pen is still in his journal, waiting for a tomorrow that never arrived. For the man who was named after a king, it was a humble moment in time, forever enshrined.

Diary, 11/25/50

38 degrees

"Windy & rainy. We had very hard winds all day lasting until midnight. It was as bad as a hurricane, there was a lot of damage done around the eastern part of the U.S. Kathryn & I went to the movies in Athol tonight."

Strength...

One of my dad's favorite sayings was: "It's a great life if you don't weaken." This was also the title of a country song by Faron Young back in the 1950s. As a young adult, my dad likely hummed along to that song while doing morning chores on the farm or driving to the grain store. Even though he was not a dancer, the beat probably made his toes wiggle a little in his barn boots. For my dad, though, it was also a piece of wisdom that he was happy to pass along every time things went sideways in life.

As a New England farmer, my dad was not much for philosophical discussions or lengthy conversations. His front porch counseling was usually limited to a few words meant to show that he had listened to you, contemplated your issue, understood, and cared. There was also, let's call it, "sweat counseling." If he knew there was an issue troubling you, he would find a physical chore that you could help him with. Thinking back, it was probably his way of getting my full attention. I could not talk and breathe hard at the same time! His best moments of imparting wisdom were normally accompanied by me breaking a sweat.

When my first marriage ended, I was young and unsure of how to move forward. Life just seemed more complicated than I'd expected. One afternoon, when I was back living with my parents, my dad asked me to help him throw firewood into the cellar. A truckload of large chunks would feed their wood furnace through icy winter days. This chore took us several hours to finish, our silence only broken by the sound of each piece hitting the cellar floor with a thud. I found it therapeutic to repeat the same motion over and over. My dad's arms, wrapped in plaid flannel, could pick up twice the number of logs that I could. When the truck was finally emptied, I felt accomplished and better about myself than I had in months. I was drenched in sweat and full of pride from a job well done when my dad offered his singular thought on my breakup: "It's a great life if you don't weaken."

To this day, I draw on that simple song and the lesson of the woodpile. I translate it to mean that even when things are difficult, you need to keep moving forward. Do not let challenging times defeat you. When my brain needs to sort through an issue, I find myself seeking a physical task with a rewarding end, just like stacking firewood. I create a garden space, cut brush, deep clean a neglected part of the house, take a long walk, or tackle a big task that seems doable. As I sweat and process, I feel my dad's presence with me. Then afterwards, like any decent daughter of a Swede, I take a well-earned Fika. As I sip my coffee, I whisper, "Thanks, Dad, it truly is a great life."

Thoughts...

*T*hese *"Thoughts" at the end of each section are a place for jour-*
naling. You can use the prompts if you choose or just let your
own thoughts flow. There is space for words, drawings, or col-
lages—let your mind create as you ponder my dad's lessons.

How do you get through tough times? Where do you find
strength? What do you do to make difficult times easier?

Remembering Gus...

"I remember at my mother's funeral, I felt a hand on my shoulder—it was [Gus's] hand. No words, and I knew what he was saying. His gentle ways were kind."

– C.A.

Kindness...

Over the years, many people have shared stories about the kindness my dad showed them. Being kind came quite easy to him, and it was not something he ever had to stop and consider. If he saw someone struggling with a chore, he would help. If he was owed money but the person was strapped financially, he would tell them to pay when they could. If it was obvious somebody was having a difficult day, he was quick to share a smile.

Growing up, there was a family down the street from us who lived life very simply. There was a mother and three adult sons all over the age of sixty. They owned a car, but no one knew how to drive, so their main mode of transportation was a bicycle. They patched their roof every time it rained and kept the front door open whenever the July humidity demanded a breeze. My siblings and I called the family poor, but that was never a verified fact. They always had money on the first of the month, but by the end of the month, they were borrowing money from my dad for food. For the sake of privacy, I'll call them the Smith family.

Every time Halloween rolled around, the Smith brothers would tell my dad that no kids ever knocked on their door.

They would speak with dismay about the neighborhood kids passing by their house without stopping. So, of course, my dad told us that if we were going to trick-or-treat, we had to stop at the Smith house. I did not want to because they always gave out a bruised apple instead of a tasty candy bar. Dad explained to me that the type of treat wasn't the point. The point was that their feelings were hurt. He went on to say that it would only take me a few minutes to stop at their house and then when I was out of sight, I could throw the apple in the bushes. My dad said kindness was the goal. I listened to him and did the kind thing, but I never ate the apple!

Many times, in the summer, Henry Smith would stop at our house with a bucket of blueberries he'd picked. He would ask my mom if she could make him a blueberry cake. Henry explained that there were enough blueberries for her to make two cakes—one for my family as well. Henry was showing kindness. By the time my mom had sorted through the berries and pulled out all the twigs, leaves, beetles, and unripe green berries, there was barely enough for one cake. The next day, my dad would deliver the cake to the Smith family. When they asked about our cake, he would tell them it was so good we'd eaten it all in one night.

My dad showed kindness. He could have told them the truth. But the truth would have accomplished only one thing—it would have hurt their feelings. The Smiths did not know that their apples went in the bushes, and they never knew that their blueberries only made one cake, but they valued kindness, just like my dad.

Kindness is a simple word with giant repercussions. Caring for someone else or something else with compassion has the potential for deep personal reward. It's a good day when you can share a smile and give joy to others. That light can be contagious, so pass it on.

Thoughts...

How do you show kindness? Do you have to think about it, or does it happen naturally? How does it make you feel when someone is kind to you? Can kindness have a ripple effect? How can you inspire others with your kindness?

Diary, 4/11/01

52 degrees

"Finished boiling sap today. We made 587 gallons for the season. It was all good flavor."

Grounding...

Not far from my childhood home is a three-span arch bridge that crosses the Connecticut River. It's well known to "leaf peepers" who take pictures of the beautiful New England foliage from every angle. Rising majestically from the river just north of the bridge is the French King Rock, which held a place of significance during the French and Indian War.

We lived on one side of the river with the county seat on the other side. Before the emergence of technology, it was common to cross the bridge weekly. Every time we crossed over the bridge, my dad would say, "Did you ever notice that every time you cross the bridge, you look down to see if the rock is there? It's always there, but it makes you feel better to KNOW it's there."

I shared this memory with my children so many times that whenever we crossed the bridge, they would repeat their grandpa's words. When my son went away to college out of state, he became homesick. With so much distance between us, weekends at home were not an option. The first time he returned, he dropped to his knees on the lawn and said, "Oh, my house is HERE. It's like Grandpa's rock; I feel better."

It's important to feel grounded. We all have times when there is so much going on in our lives that we need a rock. We need to know that no matter how much chaos there is, some things are constant. It gives us reassurance to know that some things never change.

I know many people who often take trips to the ocean, not necessarily to swim or to fish but just to *be*. They will tell me, "I just needed to go, and now I feel better." The ocean is their rock. Sitting at home, they know it's there—the tides washing the beach and the seagulls squawking. They know that no one has stolen it, but they still need to see it. They need to verify in their mind that even though their life may feel out of control, the ocean is constant. Like an anchor in a storm, it throws them a lifeline and reminds them that not everything changes.

For many of us New Englanders, the "Old Man of the Mountain" in New Hampshire was grounding—a man's solid profile jutting out of the granite stone. Driving north through the White Mountains, everyone looked for this natural rock formation and felt better when they saw it. When the landmark collapsed in 2003, it felt like the death of a friend. People gasped when they heard what happened and called each other with the news. No one could believe that this constant piece of their lives was gone. There's a beautiful park there now to commemorate it, but it's not the same.

Someday, my dad's faithful French King Rock may disappear beneath the mighty river. One day, my son's childhood home may fall back to the earth just as the Old Man of the Mountain did. Still, my father's lesson continues to be well noted by generations. It is important to find something in your life that you can return to occasionally to ground you and give you hope. We all need something constant to sustain us through changing times.

Thoughts...

What grounds you? Where do you go or what do you do when you need to 'reboot' yourself? What reassures and calms you?

Remembering Gus...

"Gus was always so friendly and so patient. He would answer every question that we had with a smile. He treated all people in this cheerful and respectful manner."

- D.W.

Faith...

My father was not a churchgoer. He did not have anything against religious services, it just wasn't how he chose to participate in prayer. Most Sunday mornings, he would finish things that needed to be done on the farm while my mom took us to church. Afterwards, we would go for a drive, which normally involved visiting relatives, and then we'd have a big Sunday lunch.

One day, I asked my dad why he didn't go to church. (The subliminal question was why I had to go and he didn't.) He told me that he could find God just as easily in a hayfield as he could at a house of worship. That has always resonated with me, and it taught me that conversations with a higher power aren't just reserved for one day a week within a certain building. They do not need to be led by someone with a degree in theology. They do not even need to have structure. My dad shared his prayers with the birds and the trees. Nature was his cathedral.

I'm not sure you can be a farmer without asking for help from above. You need the rain to make your grass in the field grow tall and then no rain after you cut it. Then, after you harvest the grass, which the sun has turned into hay, you need rain again. You need cold nights and warm days for the maple sap to flow from the trees—but not too cold and not too warm. Whether he was communicating with God, Mother Nature, the universe, or the angels, my father had faith that his crops would be bountiful.

Believing in a higher power can get us through demanding times and cultivate peace. I've cried in hospital chapels. I've sung in picturesque churches around the country. I've lit candles in historical cathedrals and prayed in missions. Even though those experiences were all unique and powerful, they are not the only places to find solace. My dad taught me that peace is found wherever you ask for it. Walking my dog in the morning gives me the quiet time to ask whoever is listening to help me solve whatever issues are spinning in my head. I have faith that some higher power will guide me to the answers.

The Good Book says you only need faith the size of a mustard seed. Our faith gets tested whether it's as tiny as a mustard seed or as big as a mountain. When one of us was having a difficult day, my dad used to say, "You just need to put one foot in front of the other." In other words, just move forward and have faith.

Many people sense something is missing in their lives. They travel around the world looking for guidance within renowned places of worship and from people with important titles. They travel thousands of miles to go on a pilgrimage. All those ways to connect with a higher being are worthy and honorable, but not they are the only way. My father discovered his peace through quiet reflection in a hay-field.

Thoughts...

Where do you find peace? How do you define faith? Do you believe in a higher power? Is it hard for you to just be still and trust in that power to guide you?

Diary, 6/30/00

71 degrees

"I found a turkey on a nest of 7 eggs, also a turkey with 8 little ones."

Respect...

As I mentioned previously, Henry Smith lived down the road from us. He was an older, uneducated man who picked up a little work wherever he could. At the end of every month, when there were more days left than there was cash, he would find my father and ask to borrow twenty dollars. My dad always gave it to him. Usually, the first week of the month, Henry would show up at our house to repay the loan. One day, I asked my dad why he took the money back when this was an ongoing occurrence. Why didn't he just tell Henry to keep it since he was going to ask for it again anyway? My dad told me it was all about respect. When he allowed Henry to pay back the loan, Henry felt proud that he could repay his debt. He felt good that he had not let my dad down. My dad created the opportunity for Henry to have self-respect.

My dad's father only had one hand. The other one was amputated due to skin cancer before I was born. Grandpa had a prosthetic made, but he was a stubborn man and comfortable prosthetics hadn't been invented yet—so he never used it. He lived a distance from town. Since my grandmother didn't have a driver's license, traveling into town was difficult. Grandpa solved this problem by adding a knob to his steering wheel. He also added knobs on his tractors so he could work the farm as easily as anyone with two hands. The knobs allowed him self-respect.

My father was a big believer in respecting others. He would be horrified at the public ridicule on social media today. My dad did not make fun of people. If he didn't agree with someone, he would quietly go about his business. He had opinions, and he would share them with people he trusted, but they were not out in the open. Bullying was something he wouldn't tolerate, and through his actions, he taught us empathy. Growing up, we shared our home and holidays with people of different races, backgrounds, and sexual orientations. We were encouraged to bring friends home, where they would be met with hospitality and kindness.

My father never marched in a protest or wrote letters to the local newspaper. It just was not who he was. But he loved that we had opinions, and if we were respectful, he encouraged us to share them any way we could. He would tell us that doing the right thing took a bit of thought; it wasn't always black and white. Through him, I learned that taking time to think and clear your head before voicing an opinion was always a good idea. Once words leave your mouth, they cannot be taken back, so give those words time in order to form a respectful response.

My father did not publicly pass judgment. He was a firm believer in the adage that "every dog has his day" and that fate would give people what they deserved. Just like Henry wouldn't rob my dad of his twenty dollars, my dad would never rob anyone of their self-respect.

Thoughts...

How do you voice your opinion without judgment? How do you feel when you're respected? How can you show others respect? Can you disagree with someone but still respect them?

Remembering Gus...

"Gus was the person you could look forward to see; he was always with a smile, and I never heard an unkind word spoken by him."

– E.P.

Authenticity...

My father was what some people would call the "real deal." What you saw was what you got. He was a big Swedish farmer with a curiosity about the world. He had high moral standards and an intolerance for pretention. He liked people who were genuine, like himself.

In my youth, if we took an out-of-town vacation, it usually involved farming. Many times, we traveled to the Amish country in Pennsylvania. We also drove to see big logging operations in northern Maine and visited farms in western New York. When your life involves agriculture, there's no room for pretention. Your harvest depends on the weather, your equipment sees more duct-tape than paint, and your shoes are always covered with mud. Farmers find more than twenty-four hours in a day and pause only to pray for more fortitude (and, of course, for Fika). The sentimental spot in their hearts, known as their grandchildren, softens their strong, hard lives.

The grandchildren in my family are no longer children—many have kids of their own. Even today, if you ask them to name the most authentic person they've ever known, they'll say their "Bumpa." They all spent time with him feeding the cows, gathering sap, riding the hay wagon, and going for drives. My dad especially loved his one-on-one drives with them. They knew if they were riding in the front seat next to Bumpa, he would pick their brain about everything. He was interested in their opinions and what they thought about the world. My father taught us all to be comfortable in our own skin.

The world came crashing down when my niece was eighteen months old. She was diagnosed with leukemia, and my sister took her sick little girl from Massachusetts to the University of Iowa for a bone marrow transplant. My mom went with them to provide moral support. When things took a turn for the worse, my dad knew he needed to go and go quickly.

Dad had never flown, so he was unsure of the customary preparation. He found a paper grocery bag in the pantry, into which he packed his clothes and his shaving kit. He wasn't thinking about what was appropriate or stylish. He was thinking about family. When my brother-in-law picked him up to go to the airport, he saw my dad standing there with the brown paper bag. My brother-in-law managed to find a small duffle bag in his trunk for my dad to use instead. We never heard the whole story of his flight; it was not a priority at the time. Imagine, though, the conversation among the flight attendants about the big farmer with the little carry-on bag. I hope they saw what we always did—a genuine father and grandfather who was not afraid to keep it real. He knew who he was, and he did not pretend to be anyone else.

My niece did not survive the cancer, and Dad spent a lot of time in the hayfield upon his return. This event was one of the hardest things we went through as a family, but my dad taught us that supporting each other was the most important thing. It did not matter that he had never flown, did not have luggage, or was out of his comfort zone. The priority was love.

Thoughts...

Do you know who you really are as a person? Do you consider yourself authentic? Do you show the world the real you? Are your thoughts influenced by others? Do you find yourself changing to accommodate the people you're with?

Remembering Gus...

"I made this birdhouse in memory of Gus—a humble, kind, and gentle man who in his own very unique way helped make our little corner of the world a much better place to live in. I believe that if we try to be good people, work hard, and take care of our families as best we can, that we will continue to honor Gus's memory. He was truly a special person."

- M.P.

Appreciating Nature...

Being a farmer means you must love the earth. It's in the job description. In fact, it is *the* job description. You must immerse yourself in every aspect of nature to earn respect for it, or you'll need to find a new career. My father taught me to love and revere everything nature holds, from the fiercest blizzard to the tiniest seed.

Like many farmers in northern New England, my dad made maple syrup. Making syrup is a nature-guided process, and it's a miracle that we're blessed with such sweet goodness. First, you must find a sugar maple tree that's the right age and size and in good health. In the spring, when the weather cooperates with warm days and cold nights, the tree produces a sweet sap. The farmer hammers a tap into the tree to extract the sap, which then flows from the tree. The tasty liquid is gathered up and boiled. To become maple syrup, it must have a precise consistency, which you measure using a hydrometer. On average, it takes forty gallons of sap to yield just one gallon of syrup. Our farm would produce, on average, seven-hundred gallons of syrup every spring. Sugaring was my dad's favorite time of the year. It was a time when friends and family gathered to witness and taste this wonder of nature. It was a time to appreciate the earth and what it gave us. Whether the harvest was good or not, year after year, my dad was amazed at the sweet gift he received from the maple trees.

My father always observed nature and shared those observations with us. Perhaps because he was color-blind, his other senses were more acute. He noticed the size and placement of bee hives. He marveled at the shape of snowdrifts and woodpecker holes. He would stop to watch a beaver build his dam or a new calf try to walk. We would get a call when he heard the screeches of porcupines or the howls of coyotes. My dad watched nature shows on television and loved nature photography. He enjoyed the sound of owls and nicknamed one near his house "Old Hooty." He found nature fascinating because it did not require explanation, over-thinking, or answers—it just *was*. Sometimes nature was simple, other times complex, but to him it was always calming. Nature provided nourishment for his soul.

"Forest bathing" is a concept that would have made my dad laugh. But it's a real thing. Japanese culture coined the term in the 1980s, though it has been around long before that. Forest bathing is a way to calm yourself by connecting with nature. You probably already do it but never gave it that specific name. When you're spending time in the woods, breathing in the wonderful smells of the trees and earth, that is forest bathing. You are surrounding all your senses with the peace of nature. In the mid-1800s, Henry David Thoreau wrote, "I went to the woods because I wished to live deliberately, to front only the essential facts of life."

There are times when stress overtakes me and my judgment is clouded. Sometimes all I need is to immerse myself in a pine forest and breathe deeply. It's my grounding place. My dad taught me that nature is healing. Connect with the earth in any way you can and appreciate the peace it shares.

Thoughts...

What is your favorite outdoor activity? How do you show appreciation for the earth? In what ways do you help the earth? Can nature change you?

Diary, 3/1/00

35 degrees

"Heard Old Hoot owl at 4:00 am over in the east, first time this year."

Abundance...

I was not born with a silver spoon in my mouth, but I never thought of us as poor. Looking back, we were rich in what mattered. My father told me, "You can have kids or money, but you can't have both!" I used to ask him if that meant he wished he'd had more money and less kids, but he'd just laugh and say, "Money doesn't matter, family does."

Growing up on our farm, we had two families to support. My grandparents lived in the farmhouse, and my parents, three siblings, and I lived in a house across the field. Money was tight. My mom always had a job or two, working around our needs. When I was little, she sold clothing and liquid embroidery paints at home parties. When my dad finished his work for the day and came home, she worked in the evenings. As we got older, she took classes and became a nurse's aide. The money and benefits were good, and she could work while we were at school.

Until I was in my teens, our house had no indoor plumbing. We had an outhouse. It was attached to the house through a woodshed, and it was really cold during the winter! You waited as long as you could before making the trip out there. A big, galvanized tub served as our bathtub. Twice a week, my mom would drag the tub into the kitchen and fill it with pitchers of hot water. The cleanest kid washed first. Being more of an "outdoorsy girl" than my sisters, I was always last! In between actual baths, a washcloth in the sink was our only option. It took years to save the money to add a bathroom to our house.

Even though I'm sure we qualified for government programs, there was only one we took advantage of that I can remember. It was called the Commodity Credit Corporation or the CCC. It supported U.S. farmers by providing food assistance. From them, we received free cheese and peanut butter in basic packaging with no brand name. It was needed and tasty. We raised our own beef and pork and did a lot of canning and freezing, using produce from our garden. The choices were limited, but we ate well. My mom created "unique" casseroles that my family still laughs about today.

My dad was a proud man who never agonized over finances. He took the government food only when it was necessary. Handouts were not a way of life but a way to get by. We didn't require much. Unlike today's world, we had few electronics, few luxuries, and fewer expectations. We enjoyed the time we spent with family, extended family, and friends. My parents played cards at home on Saturday nights with friends, and my siblings and I would pull together a game of "kick the can" with neighborhood kids. Sundays would find us all making homemade fudge, French fries, or popcorn. There was no social media and not a lot of television. My parents raised us like they had been raised. But we had an abundance of what was important.

Generosity has no economic boundaries. My father taught me that when you had a bounty of something, you needed to share it. Many times, he gave away some of his maple syrup as a "thank you" gift or donated it to the town's pancake breakfast. He would give people mulch hay for their garden, good hay for their horses, and meat from our freezer. My dad would donate his time and equipment to anyone who needed a hand. He would also get back as much as he gave, though it was never an expectation. I remember him plowing someone's driveway and getting half the payment in cash and half in homemade bread. Bread didn't pay the bills, but it did fill us up with good lessons on how to get by and on what it meant to be truly wealthy.

Thoughts...

Do you consider yourself wealthy? In what ways? Do you appreciate your wealth and share it? How have tough times shaped you? Did you learn more about yourself during challenging times or good times? In what way?

Remembering Gus...

"I have always admired Gus, for he represented the best of our independent Yankee heritage. He was a good, decent, and modest man. I am proud to have known him."

- R.C.

Work Ethic...

Few people work as hard as farmers. The number of required hours and workdays depend on the weather, the animals, the crops, and what might break that week. My father worked many hours, but time was not the only thing he gave to his job. He gave all his fortitude as well, letting his moral compass direct him. There's an expression that dates to 1700 England that says, "A job worth doing is worth doing well." I'm sure that shoveling cow poop was not on my dad's list of favorite jobs, but he did it to the best of his ability.

One of my first "real" jobs was working summers in a pen factory. All day long, I used a press to put a clip onto the barrel of a pen. I was ready to quit after day one. I told my dad that it was an awful job. It was boring, hot, and the eight-hour day lasted forever. I didn't think it was worth doing, so it was hard to do it well. My dad thought for a little while then told me I was looking at the job all wrong. I was only looking at it from my point of view rather than the big picture. He went on to say that I was a valuable cog in the wheel. Someone had given the company an order for pens with clips. The company needed to fulfill the order to make money so they could pay their workers. The workers needed to support their families. The families needed to buy food. He told me that my job was more important than I thought since I was part of that process, ensuring that everyone was being supported. I slept on that advice and went back to work the next day and then again, the day after that, and then for the rest of the summer. I was the best darn pen clip presser I could be. I whistled while I worked, counted the number of pens I made, smiled at people, and every day I felt accomplished.

I have followed my father's advice many times over the years. As I cleaned and made beds in college student housing, scrubbed toilets in offices, sold cosmetics through home parties, and washed dishes in restaurants, I remembered that I was an important cog in a wheel. I could do the job well, have a good attitude, and feel purposeful, or I could complain about it, not focus, and allow my time to feel wasted. The choice was mine.

Sometimes my dad would watch a worker, shake his head, and say, "If he put half the energy into doing his job as he does trying to get out of his job, he'd be ahead." Many of us have experienced co-workers who want a paycheck but don't want to earn it. They spend an awful lot of time looking at the clock and complaining. They're usually the same people who are miserable in other aspects of their lives. An optimistic attitude goes a long way. It's rare for someone to love their job all the time, and most of us would prefer not to need a paycheck at all. But my father taught me that when you do work—regardless of your job—decide for that hour, for that day, for that week, to be the best cog the wheel ever had!

Thoughts...

What is the best job you've ever had? What is the worst job you've ever had? Did you work just as hard at both? Do you feel you have a strong work ethic? Why? How did you learn it? What is your dream job?

Diary, 4/11/01

50 degrees

"This was the hardest year to gather sap I can ever remember due to deep snow. I have never seen so much snow on the ground when we finished sugaring in my lifetime."

Appreciation...

I magine if the only time you enjoyed life was when a big event happened or you went to a fabulous place. It's easy to feel on top of the world when you get a promotion, find yourself in Paris, or win the lottery. My father experienced none of those things, yet he found joy every day.

Being a farmer, he spent a lot of time outside. There was always something in nature that made him smile. I remember one day that he was later than normal for dinner. My mom asked him about it, and he said it took him longer to mow a field than he thought it would. He explained that he'd noticed coyote pups in the corner of the field playing, so he'd shut off his tractor and just watched them.

If you want to smile more, look for the little things.

One night, my husband and I took my dad out to dinner at a new restaurant in town. When our salads came, they were on cold plates. He got a big smile on his face and was so impressed that he asked the server about it. She told him they kept the plates in the refrigerator. That made him so happy. He talked about the cold plates for days!

Notice the trivial things.

"There is good in every day," Dad would say. "Sometimes you just have to look a little harder." We all have days when it feels like the world is against us. There are days when we feel like taking one more step or one more breath amounts to a monumental task. These are the times to look hard for a reason to smile. I remember many times when my dad would sit down at the end of the day with a big bowl of ice cream and remark on how he had been looking forward to that treat all day long. It was a little thing that often turned out to be the highlight of his day.

When my dad went hunting, I was always eager for his return. Yes, I missed him, but more importantly—at least to my eight-year-old brain—were the Life Savers. Whenever he got home, I would search his pockets for that tasty roll of wintergreen Life Saver candies, and there they always were. The smell of wintergreen still takes me back in time and makes me smile.

The little things cannot erase the big stuff, but your brain starts to weigh a little less every time it can navigate away from the bad. My dad taught me to focus on what's good in life. He would say that there will always be tough times; the difference is how you respond to them. Maybe the goodness in our day is something as simple as a cold salad plate or a Life Saver candy. Some days, that makes all the difference. It's up to each of us to make the choice to appreciate the little things.

Thoughts...

What are some small things that turn your day around?
What is a simple thing that makes you smile? How can
you create your own smiles? When does a small thing become more important?

Remembering Gus...

"I feel so honored to have known [Gus]. He was such a wonderful man. I will never forget his laugh and warmth."

— P.W.

Humility...

My father was one of the humblest people I've ever known. He believed in using manners and saying thank you. And he did many things without people even knowing. It was important to him to do what was right. He never had to be asked. He didn't need his picture in the newspaper. He wanted to do what he could, in his small way, to make the world a better place. He didn't hide his light under a bushel basket; his light was bright and far-reaching. He taught me early on that you control your own light. Other people cannot make it brighter. You are responsible for your own light and actions. My father judged only himself.

I recall a time when a "weekend farmer" in a nearby town had his barn burn down. He not only lost his barn but also the hay stored in it. My father, without being asked, brought the man hay for his horses. He didn't expect payment. He left it by the gate, and I doubt if the man ever even knew who left it. It was just one human being doing what he could for someone who needed a good deed. My dad brought his light to someone who was having a dark day.

The Wizard in *The Wizard of Oz* would have called my dad a "good deed doer." He was not a philanthropist, as he had no grandiose visions. He was not a benefactor, as he had no money to give. He was simply a humble farmer, quietly doing what needed to be done to make the world a better place. He merely let his light shine.

We lived a few miles from an old cemetery. Although there weren't a lot of burials performed there, there would still be an occasional service. Sometimes Old Man Winter was an unwelcomed guest. Many times, I remember my father putting on his red-and-black checkered wool pants, his big winter boots, and his warm hat before climbing on his tractor and driving to the cemetery to plow a wide path for the mourners. The town plowed the main road, but my father knew it would make the day easier for the grieving family if, once they parked their car, they didn't need to walk through a lot of snow. No one asked him to plow, no one paid him to do it, and perhaps no one even knew it was him. But, for him, it was the right thing to do.

My dad was a proud man, but he was not arrogant. He wasn't looking for votes, and he wasn't expecting an "atta boy." He appreciated it when someone expressed gratitude, but that was not the purpose behind his actions. Proverbs says, "With humility comes wisdom." No one is as wise as the humble man who shines his light quietly to make the world a better place.

Thoughts...

What are some things you do to make the world a better place? How can you make life easier for someone? What good deeds can you quietly do today? Do you need to be acknowledged for your kindness, or does it feel okay just knowing you did it?

Diary, 7/5/02

76 degrees

"Ted Williams died today. Kathryn and I, Ralph & Dotty Perry went to Fenway on the last day of his career. He hit a home run his last at bat. It was September 28, 1960."

Patience...

I n agriculture, there are no shortcuts to success—it takes a lot of grit. I'm not sure you can even be a farmer without having patience. As a farmer or gardener, you prepare the soil exactly right and then you plant a seed. You water that seed, you pluck out the weeds, you cross your fingers that the sun shines, and then you patiently wait and watch and have faith for a good result.

One day, my dad and I were talking about parenting, and in a roundabout way, he told me that you must have patience with children and think of them like a garden. You feed and nurture them (water), you steer them towards positive things and people (remove the weeds), teach them values (sunshine), and you watch and hope for a good result. He was not wrong. Parenting is a whole lot of crossing your fingers, having faith, and being patient.

The definition of patience is the capacity to accept troubling situations without getting angry. When I was younger, my father would put his hand on my shoulder and calmly say, "You just gotta have a little patience." Like all creatures, I like things to go smoothly. Now, when trouble comes, I have learned to redirect my frustration. I've found that long walks or chatting with a friend are helpful ways to vent. I'm always telling my kids to "breathe in through your nose and out through your mouth." My dad taught me that you cannot fix the whole world by yourself, but you can fix your piece of it. He used to say that if everyone fixed their corner of the world, it would be a better place. Be patient and show kindness and respect to your family, your neighbors, and your town. Slow down and have the patience to make things better where you can. Make a difference in your piece of the world.

One way my father would dispel his frustration was to change his perspective. Living on a farm, something always went wrong—weather, equipment, animals, crops, or more. My dad would often take an afternoon to visit a neighboring farm that always had bigger problems than our own. If my dad had a leaking roof, they'd have a missing roof. If it rained on his field of hay, a freak hailstorm had just destroyed their whole crop. You get the picture. Dad would visit and help them. When he came back, he'd always say, "Home looks so much better." By changing his perspective, he gained patience.

Whether it's with crops or our own personal problems, we all like instant gratification and quick solutions. The lesson I learned from my father was to relax, breathe, put your anger in perspective, do something good for your corner of the world, and try again. If we have patience, our seeds will grow.

Thoughts...

Do you consider yourself a patient person? Are there things that trigger your frustration? How can you change your perspective when you get angry? When you feel anxious, how do you calm yourself?

Remembering Gus...

"I guess it was just the quiet presence [Gus] had in life and perhaps the principals he stood for are just a few of the characters he exemplified to make him such a great guy."

- J.O.

Gratitude...

My father was a stickler for saying "thank you." It was an admirable trait that was passed down to him from my grandfather. When I was young and my friends and I needed a ride somewhere, my grandfather would agree to the transport on one condition—that he receive a verbal thank you. If someone did not thank him, he would never give them a ride again. I remember whispering to friends in the back seat, "Please say 'thank you' when you get out of the car." Looking back, it was a good lesson in gratitude for all of us.

My parents would occasionally manage to get away for a car trip, usually when it was raining and they couldn't get outdoor work done. My dad would pack three or four pints of his homemade maple syrup in the car in case they came across someone who needed a special thank you. Sometimes words were not enough.

One time, his maple syrup thank you became extra sweet. My father was not much for politics, and even though he stayed up to date with the news, he wasn't obsessed with it. So, it surprised all of us in 1991 when my dad said he wanted to send some of his syrup as a thank you to General Norman Schwarzkopf.

The general had recently retired following Operation Desert Storm, and my father thought he deserved to know he was appreciated as an important cog in the wheel. My brother-in-law researched his address, and my mom wrote a thank-you note to accompany the gift. Imagine our surprise a few weeks later when a handwritten thank-you note arrived for my dad from the general himself—two men who did not have much in common except they were both from a generation where manners were important.

As adults with our own homes, my siblings and I would often have our parents over for dinner. Even though my parents thanked us when they left, my dad would always call the next morning. The conversation began with "I just wanted to thank you again." He felt you could never show enough appreciation.

My father held an unwavering belief that gratitude was priceless. His words and actions always had substance behind them. Whether he simply waved at someone as thanks for letting him cross the street or shipped syrup to a four-star general for his service, he expressed his appreciation.

I remember seeing a meme that said something like: "If you're in bed and cannot sleep, count your blessings not your sheep." It's a version of the song from the movie, *White Christmas*. I have done that before, and every morning, I also thank the universe for the good things in my life. My dad felt blessed with his home, his family, and his life. He taught me to express gratitude freely and to never take anything for granted. Nothing is sweeter than a well-deserved "thank you."

Thoughts...

Do you feel like a grateful person? How do you convey that? How do you feel when you express gratitude? How do you feel when people show you their appreciation? Is gratitude humbling for you?

Diary, 2/12/01

23 degrees

"Watched train going east. It had 3 engines & 86 carloads of coal."

Laughter...

My father loved to laugh. Something would strike him as funny, and he would let out a big-old belly laugh that made his eyes shut. (Picture Santa Claus in *'Twas the Night Before Christmas!*) When he laughed, you couldn't help but laugh right along with him. It was infectious.

Old TV shows like *Hee-Haw*, *Mayberry RFD*, and *The Carol Burnett Show* always made my dad laugh. He enjoyed what you would call "good old-fashioned humor." He wasn't a fan of comedians who swore or used what my mom would call "barn talk." He laughed at the dilemmas on *Green Acres*, the antics on *The Beverly Hillbillies*, and the silly bear on *Gentle Ben*. He appreciated simple humor.

My kids remember that when my dad babysat, he always wanted to watch the Disney movie *The Fox and the Hound*. Talking animals were funny, but when the hunter's pants fell down every time he tried to shoot the fox, my dad would laugh hysterically! He would rewind that part over and over just to laugh. My children still laugh today just thinking about how hard he laughed at that scene.

The Mayo Clinic says laughter is good for your health. It helps you mentally and physically. It reduces stress and lowers blood pressure. Endorphins and positive thoughts improve your immune system. There are even laughter workshops that teach you how to laugh more. Laughter is beneficial. Social media has great videos with laughing babies, playful dogs, crazy cats, and people who get themselves into silly situations. Every morning, my husband and I find something funny on social media that we share with each other. Figure out what makes you laugh and start each day with a good chuckle. Do a good deed and help someone else to laugh.

Every fall, my dad would pack up our camper and travel to northern New Hampshire to go deer hunting with his friends. When I was older, he would include my brother on these trips. When he came home—usually with no game—we would ask about the trip. After a few years of asking, it became apparent that the time away with the guys was more about telling stories and laughing. Dad would laugh just remembering how comical it was. When he tried to relay the stories, it wasn't all that funny—apparently, you had to be there!

When you find something that makes you laugh, take a little bit of it every day. Just like the famous "spoonful of sugar" that Mary Poppins sang about, it will make you healthier and your life more delightful.

Thoughts...

What makes you laugh? How can you add more laughter into your life? How do you feel when you have a good laugh? Can laughter turn your day around? How can you share laughter with others?

Remembering Gus...

"A few weeks ago, my aunt and I were talking about people who lived in the area who you never forget... To me, Gus is one of these people that people will never forget. I will always remember him plowing for my folks and then coming in for something to eat and drink. I enjoyed seeing him and my father sitting at the kitchen table discussing the local news and what was going on at your farm. Gus always used to laugh and tell me that he never saw anyone make coffee like my father... Like so many others, I consider myself fortunate to have known Gus."

- J.S.

Happiness...

My father and I never discussed happiness at length, but anyone who spent time with him would consider him a happy person. He would always tell us to "do what made us happy" and that "life is too short to not be happy." There are frequently innovative studies showing Americans are not as happy as people in other countries. I believe it's because we all get caught up in what it means to be happy. We think too deeply about it. Happiness means different things to different people.

My dad wasn't wealthy, but he proved the old proverb true: "Money can't buy happiness." Some of the wealthiest people scowl too much. My dad found happiness in different ways every day. Sometimes it was a big happy, sometimes just a little happy, but every day brought him happiness. And he created his own happiness. When he managed to get his field of hay baled and in the barn just before it rained, he felt accomplished and happy. On holidays, when the whole family sat around the table for a meal, he was happy. He enjoyed the little things that nature showed him. The feeling of contentment made him happy. Sunday afternoons, we would make homemade ice cream with an old-fashioned wooden bucket and churn. It would take lots of ice and salt to keep it cold while we took turns churning. The treat was well worth the effort, and my dad would smile, close his eyes, and relish the taste. There was a time when he became almost obsessed with the game of croquet. We had a course set up on our lawn, and one summer we even played before breakfast! My sisters and I would play in our pajamas. Dad said it was the best way to start his day. Simple pleasures that brought him great happiness.

Many people have the misguided impression that it's up to other people to make them happy. No one else can make you happy. Other people can be concerned with your happiness, but your happiness is only controlled by yourself. Figure out what really makes you happy and content. Make a list and focus on spending more time doing those things. Little things or big things, as long as they help you smile.

Learning made my dad happy. He liked to know how things worked. When he and my mom could get away for a few days, they frequently drove to the locks on the Hudson River in New York. They would watch the ships go in and out, and he would ask the employees lots of questions. When I was little, I remember going on long drives to the New Holland factory in Pennsylvania to watch how hay balers were made. Seeing and learning new things firsthand satisfied my dad's curiosity and made him happy.

My father found what made him laugh, smile, feel contented and fulfilled. He lived in the moment and discovered what brought him peace. He created his own happiness by knowing what was good for his psyche. His "happy place" was wherever he was appreciating life. Generations of my family have benefited from my father's outlook on happiness, and his memory makes us smile.

Thoughts...

Have you discovered your happiness? How can you create your own happiness? Is your happiness different every day? Do you experience both big and little types of happiness? How are they different? Do they both bring you joy?

Diary, 10/28/01

41 degrees

"The family put on a BIG 50th anniversary party for us at the Elks Club. Had all kinds of finger rolls, pickles, dips, desserts, and everything, must have been 300 plus people there, had a great time."

Socialization...

My father did not have the gift of gab, but he mastered the art of conversing. He loved to chat with people. You're probably scratching your head at this since I've mostly described him as quiet. And he was quiet; he got voted "most quiet" in the senior superlative section of his yearbook. He appreciated silence, but he also loved to "visit."

Socializing is more than just chatter. My dad loved to sit with people on their porches, around our dining room table, or at the farm and just interact. His social time— aka, Fika—normally involved coffee, iced tea, or his favorites: a big bowl of ice cream or homemade pie. Even though his days were long, he enjoyed making time for people. He was curious about whoever he talked to and curious about life. He wanted to know what their job entailed, when their folks would be in town, where their brother was building a house, how the Red Sox expected to win the pennant with the current pitching staff, and why we seemed to have more ground-nesting bees than usual.

No matter what the topic, my dad loved to listen to other people's responses. I often wondered if he used those conversations as background noise when he drove the tractor around the field or chopped wood. Without a radio, he would replay them in his head and think about things. My dad was a deep thinker. He would have hated texting but would have loved the instant answers available these days on the internet.

Early in life, my parents would take us to visit our relative's homes. Most of the people were much older than me. They were often older than my folks. I listened to stories about relatives who had passed—"Now what year did he die?" There were memories of big storms: "Didn't his silo blow down in the hurricane of thirty-eight?" There were hours of conversations that were fascinating (not) for a kid my age. I always hoped they had a deck of cards or something to entertain myself. We would never have considered bringing along a handheld video game or (gasp) pulling out a cell phone. We were expected to listen and occasionally answer a question. We were taught to socialize. I'm sure I fell asleep occasionally, and I know I was the first one to jump up when it was time to leave, but these experiences helped me in the long run.

One of my biggest regrets in life was not taking more time to socialize with my father. At one point in my life, I was a single working mother with two kids. My kids loved to hang out at my parent's house, and many times when I picked them up, my dad would say, "Sit a minute, have a coffee." I would think of the laundry, the cooking, and the school projects that needed finishing and then tell him I would sit and visit another day. I always thought there would be plenty of time to socialize, until there wasn't.

Thoughts...

Do you enjoy being social? Do you find it is easier to connect to people on social media or in person? Why do you think that is? Is it a struggle to socialize? Are there certain people you enjoy socializing with?

Remembering Gus...

"I was deeply sad when I heard about Gus. He was one of the kindest, most genuine people that I have ever known. I always looked forward to him coming to my mill for some sawdust or a few pieces of lumber. I always made sure to take some time to talk with him, and he always made it a real pleasure. He is a man that I will never forget and will remember him by trying to be more like him."

– B.B.

Letting Go...

Christmas Day in 2002 began like most others. The kids got up early, and the wrapping paper flew in every direction. The New England air blew very cold, and the hot coffee with a touch of cinnamon tasted especially good. By mid-morning, the kids had gone to their dad's house for more fun, and my husband and I were at his family's home near Boston. Then the phone rang, and my life changed forever.

My nephew told me that my father had had a heart attack. He was at the hospital, and it was not looking good. The seventy-mile drive back home seemed endless. My brother met me at the hospital entrance to tell me that our dad had died. I was able to see him one last time and tell him I loved him as my tears washed over his cold hands. In the blink of an eye, he had become a Christmas angel.

We gathered at my parent's house, and almost immediately, food, flowers, and cards poured in. People I had not seen in years were just as devastated as we were by the loss. My father meant so much to so many people in so many ways. When it was time for his service, neither the funeral home nor the church were large enough for all the people who wished to pay their respects. My niece gave the eulogy and talked about what he would have packed in his paper grocery bag for his trip to heaven. This simple farmer had made an enormous impact on his corner of the world. His life made a difference.

One lesson my father never taught me was how to let go. As I age, I realize that *is* the lesson—I don't have to let go. I remember standing at his grave with snow on the ground, thinking, "I can't leave him here." It took me years to realize that I didn't. My dad is with me all the time. I talk to him in the morning as I walk the dog, I see him in the faces of my family, and I laugh about the qualities he shared with all of us through his "dad osmosis." The smell of Old Spice aftershave immediately transports me back to the rare times he dressed in a suit, and I smile at the memories. He lives on through my children, nieces, and nephews. Things they say or do, even their mannerisms take me to a time when he was in front of me. My dad lives on in every life he touched. His light continues to shine brightly in the lessons that he taught me. I hope his light touches you.

As I share these lessons from my father with all of you, he once again becomes bigger than life-a king, a farmer, a gentle soul with a solid perspective. A man who treated others the way he wished to be treated. I hope his lessons inspire you and sweeten your life like maple syrup. I hope they empower you like the rock in the river and fill you with the faith of a hayfield. I hope every day you find a reason to laugh.

"It's a great life if you don't weaken."

Aknowledgements

Thanks to my husband, Paul, for his years of encouragement & support to bring this book to print. A big shout out to my dear friends Paula, Chris, Jeanie, Kris & Michelle for their guidance, suggestions and edits. And forever grateful to my four children and their partners for being an endless source of inspiration. I love you all and feel blessed to have you walking the path of life beside me.

www.ingramcontent.com/pod-product-compliance
Lightning Source LLC
Chambersburg PA
CBHW020743130626
46554CB00006B/2119